My first ~

Liverpo

6th Feb 2017.

C000137657

# IMAGES OF
# LIVERPOOL

### Photographed by John Curtis

SALMON

# INTRODUCTION

From its glorious maritime heritage and diverse and spectacular architecture, to its world famous reputation for music and the arts, and the warmth of its people, Liverpool has established itself as one of the greatest and best-loved cities in the world. The part of the city from Albert Dock along the Pier Head and up to Stanley Dock, is known as Liverpool Maritime Mercantile City, and was granted the status of World Heritage Site in 2004 by UNESCO, who described the city's outstanding Waterfront as a "supreme example of a commercial port at the time of Britain's greatest global significance". Interestingly, Albert Dock includes the largest group of Grade I listed buildings in Britain.

Originally a small 12th century fishing village, Liverpool was granted a charter by King John in 1207 and soon became a major shipping port, transporting men and materials to Ireland. By the 18th century, its importance as a port grew with the trade of sugar, spice and tobacco with America, and by the time Queen Victoria came to the throne in 1837, Liverpool had become Britain's largest commercial seaport. In 1880 it was granted city status.

"I have heard of the greatness of Liverpool but the reality far surpasses the expectation." said Prince Albert in his speech at the opening of the Albert Dock in 1846. When renowned author Charles Dickens gave a speech at a banquet held in his honour at St. George's Hall in 1869, he said: "Liverpool stood foremost

*Reflections of the Port of Liverpool Building*

among the great places outside London to which I looked with eager confidence and pleasure."

Liverpool became home to hundreds of thousands of Irish citizens in the 1840s, after the Great Famine, and now also has the oldest Chinese community in Europe, and the oldest Black African community in Britain. During the early part of the 20th century, immigrants also arrived from across Europe and the Indian sub-continent, making it today the absolute epitome of a multi-cultural city.

Beyond the best-known landmarks of the city's two magnificent cathedrals and the Three Graces on the Waterfront, there are many other gems, including Sefton Park, the splendid St. George's Hall and the elegant 'Georgian Quarter'. There are many wonderful art galleries, including the Tate Liverpool, the world famous Walker Art Gallery and the Lady Lever Art Gallery at Port Sunlight. There are also numerous public works of art around the city,

including Antony Gormley's installation 'Another Place' on Crosby beach, and works by world famous artists displayed inside the Anglican Cathedral. In 2008, the city held the distinguished title of European Capital of Culture. Liverpool's international fame as the home of The Beatles and other Merseybeat bands, including Gerry and the Pacemakers, has led to its title of 'World Capital of Pop', and various music festivals and events take place around the city. The city also enjoys a reputation for excellence in classical music, via the splendid Royal Liverpool Philharmonic Orchestra, housed at the great Liverpool Philharmonic Hall, which also plays host to visiting performances by a variety of leading world musicians.

With its illustrious maritime history, outstanding musical heritage and wealth of architecture, theatre, art and museums, Liverpool is unique, and has earned its place as one of the world's greatest heritage cities.

*Albert Dock*

Beautiful sunshine on the way over but by 4.40pm had to walk through Biting rain. freezing!

### River Mersey and Waterfront

A testament to the city's importance in the 18th and 19th centuries as a principal port and centre of commerce, Liverpool's waterfront is an impressive sight, showing a wide range of architectural styles. Seen from across the River Mersey, or from the world-famous 'Ferry', the waterfront buildings include the Royal Liver Building, the Cunard Building and the Port of Liverpool Building, collectively known as the 'Three Graces'. There is also the George's Dock Ventilation Building and the ultra-modern Museum of Liverpool.

### Liver Bird, Royal Liver Building

The Royal Liver Building stands majestically at Pier Head, its twin towers surmounted by statues of Liverpool's official mascot, the Liver Bird. A reminder that cormorants were once a common sight beside the Mersey, the birds were designed by sculptor Carl Bernard Bartels, with the female looking out to sea and the male looking towards the city.

### Museum of Liverpool, Pier Head

At 8,000 square metres, the Museum of Liverpool is the country's largest newly-built national museum for a century. With more than 6,000 objects on display in a variety of galleries, the museum, which opened in 2011, tells the story of the city, and its important role in the cultural heritage of Britain.

## Albert Dock

Liverpool has a long and fascinating history as a port, and the dockland area has been redeveloped to create one of the city's busiest and most cosmopolitan heritage attractions. First opened in 1846, Albert Dock soon became a bustling centre of commerce, with cargoes arriving from all over the world. It is now a major leisure attraction with shops, restaurants and museums, including the Tate Liverpool and The Beatles Story.

### George's Dock Ventilation and Control Station

This distinctive Art Deco ventilation building was designed by architect Herbert James Rowse, to serve the first Mersey Road Tunnel, which was planned by Sir Basil Mott. Dominated by its central angular ventilation shaft, the building's design was influenced by the keen interest at the time in the art and architecture of Ancient Egypt. It is now a Grade II listed building.

### The Beatles Story, Albert Dock

Arguably the most outstanding popular music phenomenon of the 20th century, The Beatles grew up in Liverpool and will forever be associated with the city. Their success is charted in The Beatles Story, a popular visitor attraction at Albert Dock.

### Tate Liverpool

Situated within the Albert Dock complex on the waterfront, Tate Liverpool opened in 1988 and is housed in a converted warehouse. This large gallery has a diverse programme of temporary exhibitions, as well as displaying work from the Tate collection.

## Liverpool ONE

This vast shopping, residential and leisure complex in the city centre opened in 2008, the year Liverpool held the title of 'European Capital of Culture'. As well as an enormous array of shops, there are restaurants, bars and two large hotels within the 42-acre development. There are also offices, apartments and extensive leisure facilities, including a cinema, public outside spaces and an adventure golf centre. In the summer, a beach is created in Chavasse Park, complete with 240 tons of sand, a bandstand and family rides and attractions.

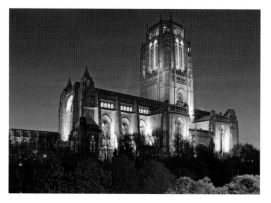

## Anglican Cathedral

The magnificent Cathedral Church of Christ, Liverpool's Anglican cathedral, stands on St. James's Mount, at one end of Hope Street, and is visible from miles around. It is the masterpiece of architect Sir Giles Gilbert Scott who, at the age of 21, won a competition called 'Design for a Twentieth Century Cathedral'. Although it was begun in 1904 and consecrated in 1924, the building of the cathedral actually continued throughout the architect's life, as he refined and changed his designs, and it was not fully completed until 1978, eighteen years after his death. Built of red sandstone in the Gothic style, the church, at 584 feet long and 198 feet wide, is the largest cathedral in Britain, and the fifth largest in the world.

Inside, the Nave Bridge, or Dulverton Bridge, was completed in 1961, unfortunately too late for the architect to see the striking new vistas he had created. The cathedral has two pipe organs, one of which is the largest in the country, and its thirteen bells, which include 'Great George', are the highest and heaviest peal in the world.

The cathedral has its own education centre, a gallery of Victorian and Edwardian ecclesiastical embroidery and a theological learning centre. There is also a fine collection of contemporary art displayed throughout the cathedral, including works by Tracey Emin, Christopher Le Brun and Elisabeth Frink, as well as 18,000 feet of stained glass, all from the 20th century.

The stained glass window opposite has a wonderful

quote. "I felt you And I Know You Loved me"

## St. James's Cemetery

Situated behind the Anglican Cathedral, St. James's Cemetery was once the site of a sandstone quarry. In 1826, architect John Foster was commissioned to design and lay it out as a cemetery, and it has now been designated by English Heritage as a Grade II Historic Park. Situated between the Oratory and the cathedral, this short tunnel lined with old gravestones is one of the entrances to the park.

## Chinatown

Home to the oldest Chinese community in Europe, Liverpool's Chinatown is situated close to the Anglican Cathedral. This colourful arch, which marks the gateway, was opened in 2000 and is the largest multiple-span arch of its kind outside of China. It was built by workers who came over from Shanghai, which is one of Liverpool's twin cities.

## Rodney Street and Canning Street

During the 18th and 19th centuries, when Liverpool flourished as a centre of commerce, elegant houses were built for the wealthy merchants of the town. In what is often referred to as the 'Georgian Quarter', Rodney Street and Canning Street contain some fine examples of architecture from this era of prosperity.

Rodney Street, laid out in the 1780s, is named after the naval commander Lord Rodney. Several buildings in this street are associated with notable people; for example, number 62 was the birthplace of William Gladstone, who served as Prime Minister four times during Queen Victoria's reign. At number 84, a handsome red-bricked building, is Watkin House, where the pioneering orthodontist Harold Watkin set up practice in 1930.

Canning Street, with its distinctive architectural features such as Ionic porticoes and iron balconies, was built between 1835 and 1845. It is named after Sir George Canning, a Liberal politician who also gave his name to Canning Dock.

## Philharmonic Hall

On Hope Street stands the Philharmonic Hall, a striking Art Deco building which plays an important part in the cultural life of the city. It rose from the ashes of the original Philharmonic Hall, which was built in 1849 and destroyed by fire in 1933. Designed by Herbert James Rowse, the new hall was officially opened in 1939. It is the home of the Royal Liverpool Philharmonic Orchestra, Britain's oldest surviving professional symphony orchestra, which was established in 1840.

## Philharmonic Hotel

The Philharmonic Hotel, known locally as the 'Phil', is an Art Nouveau building, which was designed by Walter Thomas, and is renowned for its lavishly decorated interior. The Beatles used to visit this pub, and John Lennon once remarked that one of the prices of fame was "not being able to go to the Phil for a drink".

## Metropolitan Cathedral

Liverpool is renowned for having two cathedrals, which are situated at either end of Hope Street. The Metropolitan Cathedral of Christ the King, the city's Roman Catholic cathedral, was designed by Sir Frederick Gibberd and completed in 1967. Built to an unusual circular design with the altar in the centre, the cathedral has a spectacular interior which is enhanced by the effects of light shining through the stained glass windows. The building features a lantern tower surmounted by sixteen pinnacles, representing Christ's crown of thorns.

### Abercromby Square

Named in honour of Sir Ralph Abercromby, who commanded the British army in Egypt, this square was home to wealthy merchants during the 19th century. Now part of the University of Liverpool, the square has a garden featuring a central gazebo.

### Victoria Building

Founded in 1881, the University of Liverpool is the oldest of the city's three universities. The Victoria Building, situated on Brownlow Hill, was opened in 1892 and inspired the term 'redbrick university'. It now houses the Victoria Gallery and Museum.

## 'The Spirit of Liverpool Resurgent'

This 18-feet-high bronze sculpture by Sir Jacob Epstein stands over the Ranelagh Place entrance to the former Lewis's department store, which opened in 1856 and ceased trading in 2010. Unveiled in 1956, the sculpture celebrates the resurgence of Liverpool after the Second World War, when many buildings, including Lewis's, were damaged during air raids on the city.

## Adelphi Hotel

Situated on Ranelagh Place, the Adelphi is believed to be the largest hotel in Liverpool, with more than 400 guest bedrooms. Famous people who have stayed here include Franklin D. Roosevelt and Sir Winston Churchill. The hotel features a suite which is a replica of the first class smoking lounge on the *Titanic*.

### North Western Hotel and Lime Street Station

Originally built to serve Lime Street station, the North Western Hotel was designed by Sir Alfred Waterhouse and opened in 1871. It closed in 1933, and in the 1990s it was converted into a hall of residence for students at John Moores University. Adjacent to the former hotel is Lime Street station, the largest railway station in the city centre. It was first opened to the public in 1836, and two huge iron and glass roofs were added in later decades. The roofs remain today as remarkable examples of the scale and ingenuity of Victorian architecture.

### St. George's Hall

Situated opposite the former North Western Hotel, this magnificent Victorian neoclassical building was designed by Harvey Lonsdale Elmes. The entrance to the hall features a portico of sixteen Corinthian columns and, on the steps in front, a bronze statue of Sir Benjamin Disraeli, Queen Victoria's favourite Prime Minister. The statue, by Charles Bell Birch, was erected in 1883.

### Cenotaph, St. George's Plateau

Situated in front of St. George's Hall, like an altar in front of a Greek temple, the Cenotaph is a war memorial which was unveiled in 1930. Designed by Lionel Bailey Budden, the Cenotaph has two sculpted bronze reliefs by George Herbert Tyson Smith, one of a marching army and the other depicting a commemoration of Armistice Day.

... A GREAT COMPANY · A...

### St. John's Gardens

Lying to the west of St. George's Hall, these gardens were created at the beginning of the 20th century on a site previously occupied by a church and a cemetery. The gardens contain seven statues, six dedicated to politicians and philanthropists who were influential in Liverpool during the 19th century, and one commemorating the South African War.

### Statue of Queen Victoria

On St. George's Plateau, in front of St. George's Hall, are two impressive equestrian statues by Thomas Thornycroft of Queen Victoria, and her husband, Prince Albert. Sculpted in bronze and mounted on a granite pedestal, the statue of the queen was unveiled in 1870. Queen Victoria conferred city status on Liverpool in 1880.

## William Brown Library and Museum

Designed by Thomas Allom and opened in 1860,
this grand neoclassical building stands on land
which was originally donated by Sir William
Brown, a wealthy merchant, banker and politician.
Today, the building houses part of the World
Museum and the Central Library. It is part of
the William Brown Street Conservation Area,
the principal cultural quarter of Liverpool.

## Walker Art Gallery

Situated on William Brown Street, this gallery is
named after its main benefactor, Sir Andrew
Barclay Walker. It opened in 1877, and is home to
one of Europe's finest collections of paintings and
sculpture. On either side of the entrance are
statues by John Warrington Wood of Italian
Renaissance artists Michaelangelo and Raphael.

## King George V and Queen Mary

These bronze statues, both more than nine feet high, are located at the entrance to the Queensway Tunnel, otherwise known as the 'Mersey Tunnel' or the 'Birkenhead Tunnel'. The figures were created in honour of King George V, who reigned from 1910 to 1936, and his wife, Queen Mary. The royal couple visited Liverpool in 1934 and opened the Queensway Tunnel beneath the River Mersey, then the longest underwater tunnel in the world, connecting the city with Birkenhead, on the Wirral peninsula. The opening ceremony was watched by some 200,000 people. Following the death of King George V in 1936, Sir William Goscombe John was commissioned to make statues of the king and queen. These were cast in bronze by A.B. Burton, and unveiled in 1939. The statues, which have been repositioned twice over the years, were rededicated in 1994 by Prince Edward, Duke of Kent, to commemorate the 60th anniversary of the Queensway Tunnel.

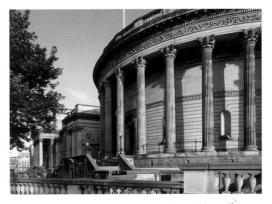

## Picton Library

Designed by Cornelius Sherlock and completed in 1879, this circular building was nicknamed 'Picton's Gasometer' in Victorian times. It is named after Sir James Picton, chairman of the Libraries and Museums Committee, who laid the foundation stone. The Picton Library, also known as the 'Picton Reading Room', was the first public building in Liverpool to have electric lighting. It is now part of the Central Library, on William Brown Street.

**Bluecoat Chambers**

This Grade I listed, Queen Anne style building was originally built in the early 18th century as a school for poor boys. The school moved to larger premises in 1906, and the building is now a flourishing centre for creative arts, known as the 'Bluecoat'.

**Church of St. Luke**

Gutted by fire in May 1941 after being hit by an incendiary bomb, this church stands as a reminder of the destruction caused by air raids on Liverpool during the Second World War. The bombed-out church was reopened to the public in 2007.

# THE CAVERN CLUB

## THE CAVERN
### LIVERPOOL
www.cavernclub.org

THE CAVERN

THE CAVERN

CAVERN CLUB OPENING HOURS

MONDAY        10 .30am - 12 .30am
TUESDAY       10 .30am - 12 .30am
WEDNESDAY     10 .30am - 12 .30am
THURSDAY      10 .30am - 2 .00am
FRIDAY        10 .30am - 2 .00am
SATURDAY      10 .30am - 2 .00am
SUNDAY        10 .30am - MIDNIGHT

Polite Notice

We Welcome Families
Until 7pm

No Minors Under 18
on The Premises After
9pm

## Cavern Club

This legendary club, on Mathew Street, originally opened as a jazz venue in 1957. It was here that Brian Epstein, manager of The Beatles during the 1960s, first heard the group play. The club thrives as a live music venue and as a visitor attraction.

## Queen Avenue

This picturesque narrow side-street, lined by shops and offices, is situated between the thoroughfares of Castle Street and Dale Street, in the traditional business quarter of Liverpool. It is part of the Castle Street Conservation Area, where there are numerous historic buildings associated with banking and insurance.

### Castle Street

The name of this street serves as a reminder that Liverpool once had a castle, which was built in the 13th century and demolished in the 18th century. Castle Street contains some of the city's finest examples of Georgian and Victorian architecture.

### Derby Square

The focal point of this large open space is a splendid monument to Queen Victoria. Designed by Charles John Allen, it was unveiled in 1906. The monument bears a plaque with the words: "On this site formerly stood the castle of Liverpool".

## Town Hall

Described by English Heritage as "one of the finest surviving town halls of the 18th century", this magnificent Grade I listed building, on Castle Street, is a masterpiece of Georgian architecture. It was originally built between 1749 and 1754 to a design by John Wood. The dome was designed by James Wyatt in 1802 after a major fire; on top of it stands a statue by Felix Rossi, of Minerva, the Roman goddess of wisdom.

## Dale Street

Part of the Castle Street Conservation Area, this thoroughfare was once the main route into and out of Liverpool from London and Manchester. Dale Street has an eclectic array of buildings dating from the Victorian era. One of the most striking is the red-bricked Prudential Assurance Building, designed by Sir Alfred Waterhouse.

## India Buildings

Built by well-travelled architect Herbert Rowse between 1924 and 1932, India Buildings is a vast office block on Water Street, in the heart of the business and financial quarter of the city. Originally designed so that it could be transformed into a warehouse, it is now home to a stylish shopping arcade, as well as barristers' chambers, modern offices and local government departments.

## Exchange Flags

Once the site of the Liverpool Cotton Exchange, Exchange Flags is a large square which is enclosed by Liverpool Town Hall, right in the heart of the city's commercial district. To the north of the town hall the bronze Nelson Monument, designed by Matthew Cotes Wyatt, was unveiled in 1813, and is considered to be Liverpool's first major sculpture.

## Oriel Chambers

Designed by Peter Ellis and built in 1864, Oriel
Chambers stands on the corner of Water Street
and Covent Garden. With its cast-iron frame and
protruding oriel windows, this building has had a
strong influence on the design of office buildings
across the world, and is said to have inspired some
of the early Chicago skyscrapers, as well as the
distinctive New York skyline we see today.

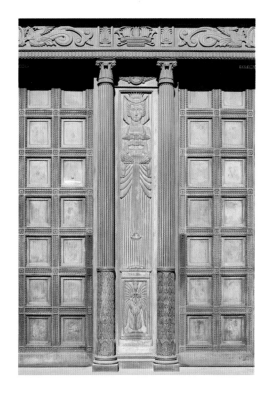

## Martins Bank Building

Finished in 1932, and designed by Herbert Rowse, one
of the most influential Liverpool-based architects of
the inter-war years, Martins Bank, once the Bank of
Liverpool, was acquired by Barclays Bank in 1969.
This impressive Grade II listed building stands on
Water Street, in the centre of Liverpool's financial
district, but is no longer a bank.

### Sefton Park

Some two miles from the city centre lies the picturesque, 200-acre Sefton Park, where in spring daffodils bloom beside the lake in Marie Curie Cancer Care's 'Field of Hope'. The park also features a magnificent Palm House, which was built with funds donated by Liverpool millionaire Henry Yates Thompson, and opened in 1896. The cast iron, Grade II listed Victorian glasshouse holds a fine collection of tropical and exotic plants and several statues, including one of the naturalist and author Charles Darwin, a keen plant collector.

## 251 Menlove Avenue

Bought by Yoko Ono and donated by her to The National Trust, 'Mendips', or 251 Menlove Avenue, was the childhood home of John Lennon. This semi-detached 1930s house belonged to Lennon's Aunt Mimi, who took over his upbringing when he was five years old. The house has been restored to the style of the 1950s, and is now open to the public.

## Strawberry Field

Once a Salvation Army children's home, the name of Strawberry Field became world famous after John Lennon wrote the song entitled 'Strawberry Fields Forever' for The Beatles. The children's home was near where Lennon lived and, as a child, he would go with his Aunt Mimi, to their annual garden party.

## 20 Forthlin Road

Some of the earliest Beatles songs were composed and rehearsed in this ordinary terraced house, where singer Paul McCartney lived before his rise to fame as part of the 'Fab Four'. Now owned by The National Trust, 20 Forthlin Road is a popular attraction with large numbers of Beatles fans from all over the world.

## Speke Hall

Standing in a wooded park beside the River Mersey, Speke Hall is one of the best-known half-timbered houses in the country. Now owned by The National Trust, it is an intriguing combination of Tudor construction, with Victorian interior decoration and domestic equipment.

### Croxteth Hall

Originally built in 1575, Croxteth Hall was home to the Molyneux family, the Earls of Sefton, until the death of the last earl in 1972. The Grade II listed building and its beautiful surrounding parkland are now owned by Liverpool City Council.

### 'Another Place', Crosby Beach

Antony Gormley's evocative sculptures on Crosby Beach create life-like silhouettes against the setting sun. The installation 'Another Place' is a collection of 100 cast-iron figures looking out to sea, each one a cast replica of the artist's own body.

## Birkenhead

Situated on the west bank of the Mersey, Birkenhead sits opposite Liverpool, on the Wirral peninsula. Formerly Birkenhead Town Hall, this fine building in Hamilton Square has also been the Wirral Museum, and is the town's register office. Said to have provided inspiration for the layout of Central Park in New York, Birkenhead Park was the first publicly funded park in Britain. It was designed in 1843 by Joseph Paxton as the forerunner of the Parks Movement, creating public open spaces for the welfare of the populace.